50 GREAT Make-it, Take-it Projects

LaBritta Gilbert

UpstartBooks

Fort Atkinson, Wisconsin

With deepest appreciation to:

Kathey, for your belief in this book and your expert word processing that made it one. I couldn't have done it without you;

Michael, for your beautiful photographs that gave my projects life;

Wayne and Russell, for always being available for computer help when I needed it;

bill, for pronouncing these projects worthy of teachers and children; I set my standards by your measure.

PARENT
TEACHER
745.5
GIL

Published by **UpstartBooks**
W5527 Highway 106
P.O. Box 800
Fort Atkinson, Wisconsin 53538-0800
1-800-448-4887

© LaBritta Gilbert, 2002
Cover design: Heidi Green; Project photography: Michael Gilbert.

The paper used in this publication meets the minimum requirements of American National Standard for Information Science — Permanence of Paper for Printed Library Material. ANSI/NISO Z39.48-1992.

Contents

Introduction

My class was preparing to make "Stuffed Animals," one of my favorite projects. I carefully set the stage by asking for their suggestions for the kinds of animals that would work best for this project. High on their lists were horses and giraffes. I pointed out the difficulty those animals' long, thin legs might present, and eventually, we settled (or so I thought) on plump kinds of animals—pigs, ducks, turtles, rhinos, dinosaurs. Imagine my surprise—and delight—at the smiling, flower-bedecked snake one student made, following her vision, not mine. I thought it couldn't possibly work, but, luckily, she knew otherwise. Another student's portrayal of a tiger was equally striking: a handsome striped face and no body—he didn't think it needed one. Of course, it didn't. Art teachers live for this kind of originality and serendipity—creations springing to life, filling a room and enchanting it.

Liberating Little Artists

Ah, child art! What could be better than helping children do what they love doing—making things with their own hands?

Good child art engages minds and imaginations as well as hands; children see materials not as they are, but as they can make them. It leaves plenty of room for choice, so it will bear its creator's imprint. It invites them to use both orthodox and unorthodox materials: to learn what those materials will and won't do, how to cooperate with them, how to make them fulfill their visions.

Our goal is not to produce artists but to liberate them—every child has an artist within—and gumdrop sculptures are as good a way as any to do this. (If art can't be fun, what can it be?) Not only can (and should) it be fun, it can be simple, and elegantly so. Colorful, clean-lined projects that are alive with movement are within every

teacher's and student's reach. That describes the projects in this book. Each one contains a surprise—either an unfamiliar material or a new way of using a familiar material. Items as diverse as index cards (what a bonanza for art teachers), discards and grocery items come together in unexpected and altogether pleasing ways.

When your students were younger, their art consisted largely of experiencing the creative process and experimenting with materials. Now they want (and need) to produce things—things they can plan and execute, see through to completion. Experimentation is an important first step in some of these projects, but it always leads to finished products. Expect your students to apply the same thought and planning to marshmallow sculptures as they do to marker graphics.

How to Use this Book

Whether you are preparing for storytime at a public library, class time in a library media center or creating project bags for children to take home and do with their parents, *50 Great Make-it, Take-it Projects* has lots to offer you.

We have grouped the projects by type, placing all the structures together, all the lettering together, etc. Among the groupings, you'll find some projects more challenging than others. Suggested grade levels are listed with each project in the Table of Contents. Some projects are more easily adapted for project bags, while others require direct, knowledgeable supervision. All of them are sure to bring out the creativity and uniqueness of every child.

Color plates of each project follow this Introduction. The plates are labeled with the project name and page number. Similarly, each project page includes a black and white photo of the project.

Each project page begins with a brief introduction, usually followed by preparation instructions, unless none are needed. Next is a list of necessary supplies and a photo of the finished project. Lastly, directions to the student are written in clear, step-by-step points, and are suitable for photocopying and class distribution.

Supplies and Sources

The supplies for these projects are easy to find and inexpensive. You probably already have many of them. The following is a list of supplies to make the projects and where to get them.

Miscellaneous

- Index cards—3 ½" x 5" for most of the projects requiring them; 4" x 6" size for one project; white and colored, unruled on both sides. Order them from school supply catalogs in five bright (preferable) or light colors: pink, orange, yellow, green, blue.

- Art tissue—from school supply catalogs; possibly from craft stores; either the non-bleed or bleed variety in packages of 20 assorted colors (lasts a long time; a good investment).

- Styrofoam—a material with many possibilities, easy for children of any age to work with. Supermarket butchers will usually order a supply of 200 or so meat trays inexpensively for you or you can buy them from a grocer supply listed in the phone book yellow pages. Get white and as many colors as you can—blue, pink, yellow and black are common. Most any thickness will work, but the thinner ones are better with student scissors. Any size will do; approximately 8" x 10" is a common size and works well. Cut the sides away with scissors or a paper trimmer, leaving flat surfaces (indentations are fine) before class time.

- Matte board—this heavyweight backing is needed for several projects; a basic art material with many uses. Ask a picture framer to save matte-board scraps for you; they will be large

pieces in a wide array of colors and inexpensive. Some framers donate them to schools. Cut matte board with a paper trimmer (adult scissors will also cut it; student scissors won't).

- Straws—colored plastic drinking straws, about 8" long, from grocers, craft stores and party shops. Get the straight, not flexible, kind.

- Yarn—leftover yarn from needlecraft projects, etc., will work or you can buy it; most any kind, colors and weights will do. Prepare it before children use it: either roll it into balls, insert the balls in small self-sealing plastic bags, cut a corner off and let children pull the yarn out the hole or wind it on empty bathroom tissue tubes with a slit cut in the edge for the yarn end.

- Ribbon—from fabric and craft stores; get as many colors, widths, patterns and textures as you can. Cut it into long lengths the children can cut from.

- Medicine droppers—supermarkets or drug stores sell these. Get plastic ones of any size; students share them.

- Bathroom tissue cardboard tubes—students can bring them from home.

- Lightweight cardboard—most any kind will do, cereal box weight.

- Small cups or muffin tins for holding water.

- Clear or translucent bottles—about ½ cup capacity; spoons—one-ounce measures or small scoops; see the "Salt" project for details.

- Newspapers.

Grocery Items

- Sugar cubes—in one-pound boxes.

- Apples, oranges, acorn squash.

- Pasta—lasagna, rigatoni, fettuccine.

- Marshmallows—large size, white or colored.

- Gumdrops—large or small (the small size are called spice drops).

- Salt—most economical in four-pound boxes as canning and pickling salt.

- Wood ice cream/frozen treat sticks—recycled ones will be fine or you can buy them as craft sticks in craft stores or school supply catalogs.

- Wood (bamboo) skewers—6" length, in housewares sections.

- Wood or plastic toothpicks.

- Wood coffee stirrers—about 5 ½" long, in the coffee section of the grocery store.

- Food coloring in dropper (squeeze) bottles—four colors: red, blue, green, yellow.

- Large paper grocery bags (or brown craft paper).

- Paper towels—white, unprinted.

- Small self-sealing (sandwich size) plastic bags.

School Supplies

- Colored construction paper— 9" x 12" and 12" x 18", in assorted colors (at least red, blue, green, yellow, purple, orange, pink, black and brown—others optional).

- White construction paper—9" x 12" and 12" x 18". Other white art paper can be used but is more expensive. Note: newsprint and manila paper will not work for any of the projects.

- Paint—good quality liquid (not powder) tempera (don't dilute); in at least red, blue, green, yellow, brown, black and white; twice as much black and white as colors. Other colors—violet, magenta, turquoise, orange if possible, particularly for upper grade levels.

- Paint cups, palettes or paper plates for mixing paint.

- Paint mixing sticks (or craft sticks).

- Markers—broad-line, non-toxic, children's markers in assorted colors—red, blue, green, yellow, orange, purple, black, brown; others optional. Be sure they flow well and the tips are in good condition.

- Scissors—good quality, pointed or semi-pointed. Be sure these work well (try them yourself).

- Glue—any school glue will work for the paper and index card projects; only white school glue (not gel) will work for the tissue and sugar-cube projects. If bottles are clogged, pour the glue into containers and students can apply it with brushes.

- Brushes—a set for paint and a set for glue; flat, approximately ½" wide for both. (Mark one set to distinguish it from the other; using brushes with glue will make them unusable for paint.) Get glue completely out of brushes.

- Rulers (yardsticks and meter sticks optional but a good idea).

- Paper hole punches.

- Paper clips.

- Clear cellophane tape (masking tape optional).

- White copier or typing paper.

- String.

- Pencils and erasers.

- Posterboard—22" x 28" sheets in several colors and black and white.

- Graph (squared) paper—wherever school supplies are sold.

Help your class become conscientious paper scrap savers: place containers nearby during all projects that use construction paper and tissue and let them put large and medium-sized scraps in them. Use them later for projects that don't require full sheets.

The processes for making some of the projects may be new to you, so you'll want to try them yourself first. You may need to make some from start to finish—you'll know which; trying the first steps or processes of others will be enough. Also, you may want to repeat projects during the year, using the suggested variations or your own.

A word of caution: to avoid unduly influencing your students in their choices and interpretations, don't show them models or pictures of the projects.

Color Plates

3D Structures and Sculptures

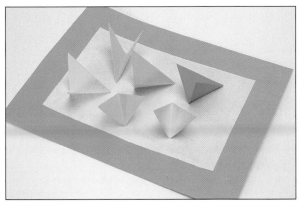

Butterflies p. 17

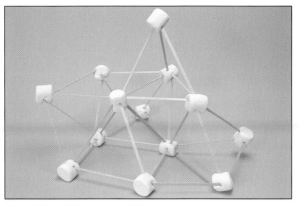

Marshmallows p. 21

Gumdrops p. 18

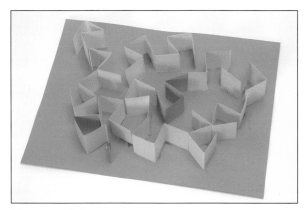

Maze p. 22

Lasagna p. 19

Pop-Ups p. 23

9

3D Structures and Sculptures cont.

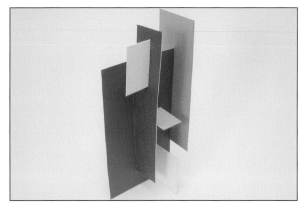

Rectangles p. 24

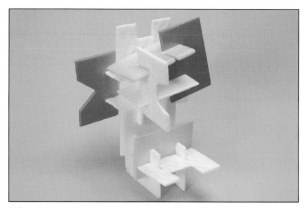

Skyscrapers p. 28

Salt p. 25

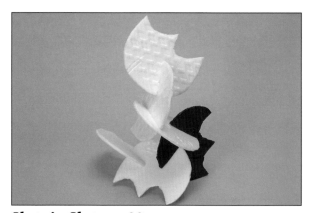

Slots in Slots p. 29

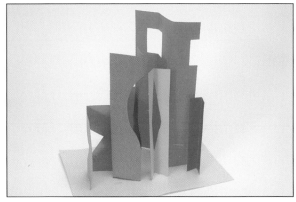

Six Standing p. 27

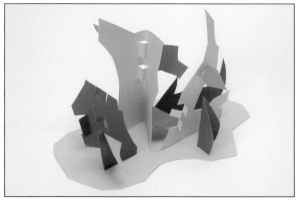

Stick-Ups p. 30

3D Structures and Sculptures cont.

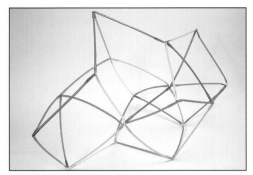

Straws and Clips p. 31

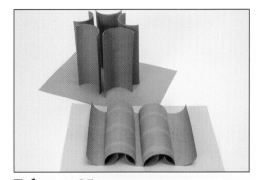

Tubes p. 35

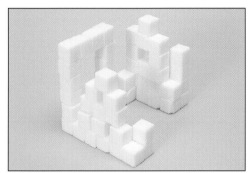

Sugar Cubes p. 32

Wee Boxes p. 36

Sugar Cube Mosaics p. 33

Wings p. 37

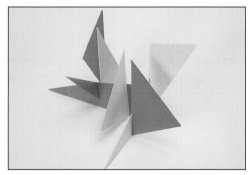

Triangles p. 34

Fabrics and Weaves

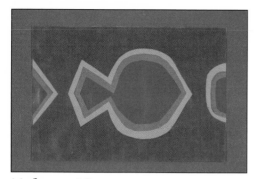

Molas p. 38

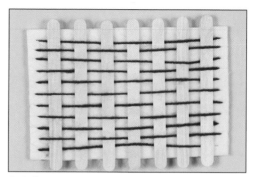

Sticks p. 41

Paper Weave p. 39

Straws p. 42

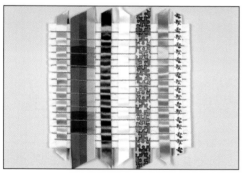

Ribbons p. 40

Mobiles and Hanging Art

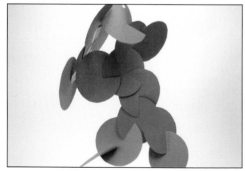

Discs p. 43

Lanterns p. 44

Mobiles and Hanging Art cont.

Mystery Mobiles p. 45

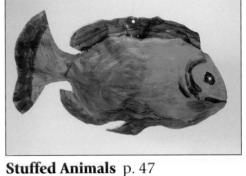

Stuffed Animals p. 47

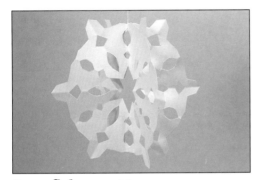

Snowflakes p. 46

2D Compositions and Paintings

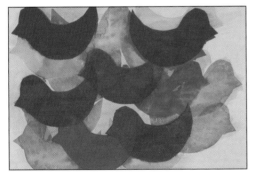

Birds p. 48

Confetti p. 51

Cityscapes p. 49

Diamonds p. 52

2D Compositions and Paintings cont.

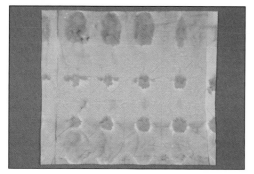

Dips p. 53

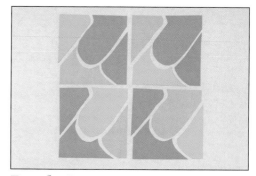

Four by Four p. 58

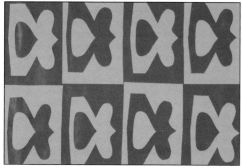

Doubles p. 55

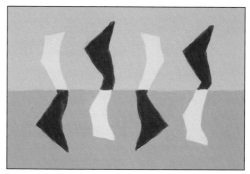

One Color p. 59

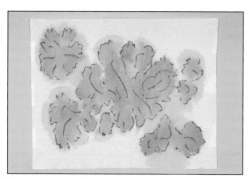

Drops p. 56

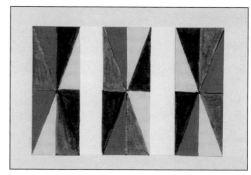

Prisms p. 60

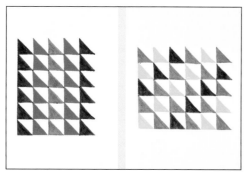

Flags p. 57

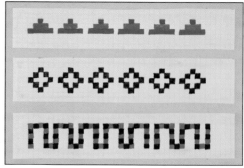

Squares p. 61

2D Compositions and Paintings cont.

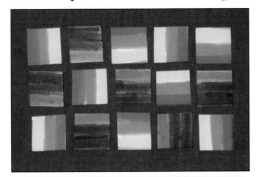

Stripes p. 62

Windows p. 64

Prints

Apples p. 65

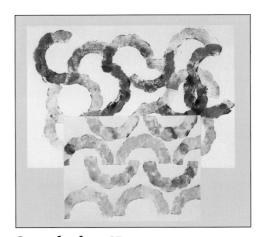

Squashed p. 67

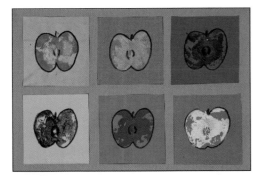

Oranges p. 66

Letters and Lettering

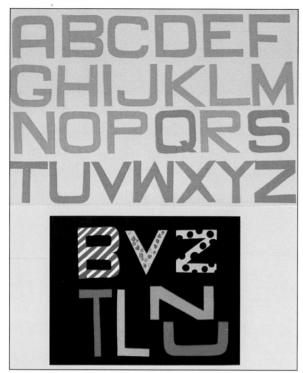

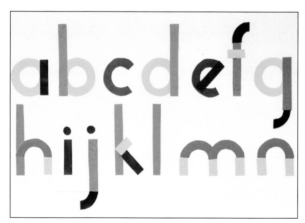

Cut Letters p. 68

Lettering p. 72

Posters p. 74

Fun & Fancy Letters p. 70

Butterflies

These easy little index-card sculptures could cap a story or study of butterflies. Students learn how to cut a square from a rectangle and how to fold, matching corners.

Preparation Instructions: Each student needs a half-sheet (cut crosswise) of 9" x 12" white construction paper, a full sheet in a color compatible with the index card colors and a little glue on a paper scrap.

What You'll Need

- Construction paper, white and colored, 9" x 12"

- Index cards, assorted colors, unruled, 3" x 5"

- Pencils

- School glue

- Scissors

Directions

◆ Share five to seven index cards of mixed colors, any combination, with another student. Fold them diagonally, bringing one short end to one long side, edges exactly even, and cut the bottom off.

◆ Cut on the folds, making two triangles, then fold these in half. You won't use the small cut ends of the cards. Each of you should use half of the triangles—five to seven each.

◆ Glue the white half-sheet to the colored full sheet, and write your name on the full sheet.

◆ Dip the folds of the cards in the glue, and set them gently on the white paper.

 © 2002, LaBritta Gilbert, UpstartBooks

Gumdrops

Children really eat this project up. Have them start with clean hands and work surfaces. You'll find skewers in supermarket housewares sections.

Preparation Instructions: Students can work singly or in pairs, particularly on small sculptures of toothpicks and small gumdrops, or in groups with gumdrops of either size. Large gumdrops and skewers make large sculptures, so be sure you have adequate space for them.

Have students begin by experimenting with forms: squares, triangles, cubes, pyramids, pentagons, etc., then make a sculpture, either incorporating the forms or taking them apart and beginning anew. Help them see parts that need shoring up or when skewers are left dangling. Give appropriate safety precautions for the toothpicks and skewers, which have sharp points.

What You'll Need

- 6" Bamboo skewers for large gumdrops

- Gumdrop candies, large or small

- Masking tape (optional)

- Pencils

- Wood or plastic toothpicks for small gumdrops

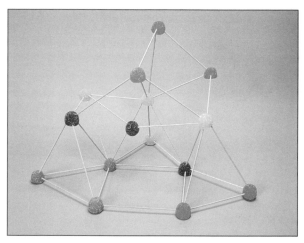

Directions

◆ Stick skewers and large candies together. Or, stick toothpicks and small candies together. Or, do both.

◆ You can put your name on the sculpture with masking tape.

Lasagna

Pasta comes in such interesting shapes—these sculptures are made with three: lasagna, fettuccine and rigatoni. Don't make them on newspaper or other paper, or they'll stick to it.

Preparation Instructions: Students need a little glue on scrap paper. During the activity while the rigatoni sets a bit—about five minutes or so—chat about pasta with the class (everybody's favorite kind, everybody's ideas about why it's made in so many shapes, what it's made of).

What You'll Need

- Lasagna, fettuccine and rigatoni
- Pencils
- School glue

Directions

◆ To start, break a lasagna strip or two into pieces—you need about three or four medium-to-large pieces and several small-to-tiny ones.

◆ Dip one end of two or three (or more) rigatoni tubes in glue and stick them on some of the larger lasagna pieces, with the lasagna lying flat. If some of the rigatoni won't stand, try others—some will work better than others.

◆ When the rigatoni pieces have dried somewhat, stick three or four of the large lasagna (with rigatoni on them, handling them carefully) pieces together. Only the ruffled and unbroken lasagna edges can stick to other pieces; broken edges are too uneven.

◆ Dip a ruffled or unbroken edge of the piece in the glue on the paper scrap or apply glue directly from a bottle (you'll need to use plenty of glue) and stick it at right angles to another piece which is standing on its ruffled or unbroken edge on the work surface.

◆ With one hand behind the standing piece and one hand holding the piece with glue on it, press the pieces firmly together and hold a few seconds, then release. Add a large or medium lasagna piece or two on the reverse side the same way, not necessarily directly opposite the one on the front side. Stick small and tiny lasagna pieces on the pieces.

◆ To finish, break a strip or two of fettuccine into pieces and stick them on the sculpture either vertically or horizontally. Write your name or initials with pencil somewhere on the sculpture and let it dry in place.

Marshmallows

Students need clean hands and workspaces for these constructions, because they tend to sample their supplies. The structures can't be made very tall, but they spread swiftly, so have plenty of supplies and plenty of space.

Preparation Instructions: Decide whether you would like students to work alone or in pairs. Discuss with them how they can make squares, triangles, five-, six- and eight-sided figures, cubes, pyramids, domes, etc.

Suggest students combine their structures in two-tier formations (marshmallows won't support much height). If space allows, make a gigantic, table-sized sculpture with the whole group.

What You'll Need

- Large marshmallows
- Wood coffee stirrers, about 5½" long

Directions

◆ Stick marshmallows and stirrers together to create shapes.

◆ Attach your shape to another student's shape to create a larger structure.

Maze

Some children may know what a maze is; others may not. Most have worked maze puzzles. These easy index-card sculptures look like mazes, but don't have entrances and exits or paths through them. They take on different dimensions when they're displayed on a wall.

Preparation Instructions: Students need a little glue on paper scraps.

What You'll Need

- Construction paper, white and colored, 9" x 12"

- Index cards, assorted colors, unruled, 3" x 5"

- School glue

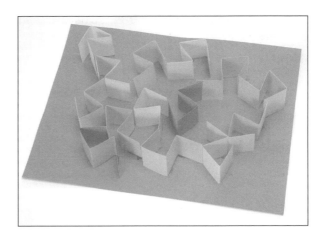

Directions

◆ Fold seven index cards in your choice of colors in half lengthwise, unfold and cut on the creases.

◆ Fold the pieces in half and in half again, crosswise, matching the corners carefully and pressing the folds well, then partially unfold them.

◆ Without using glue, stand one of the long edges on white or colored construction paper (your choice), close together or end to end, then pick each card up, dip its bottom edge in glue and set it back in place.

◆ Repeat this process until all cards are attached.

Pop-Ups

Students make these index-card sculptures lying flat and they take shape when they're "popped-up." They're made of easy-to-cut, free-form shapes.

What You'll Need

- Clear tape
- Index cards, assorted colors, unruled, 3" x 5"
- Pencils
- Scissors

Directions

◆ Without drawing, cut each of three index cards of the same color or different colors—your choice—into three or four different-sized free-form shapes. You should now have nine to twelve pieces. Write your name on one.

◆ Cut slits into each piece about one-third of the way. With the pieces lying flat on the work surface, fit the edges—not slits—of some pieces into the slits of others and put tape over the slits.

◆ When all the pieces are joined and taped (you can tape the last slit closed if you want), bend the taped parts up and coax the sculpture into a standing shape, placing it in different orientations to find the best one. It may take several times to find its best shape.

Rectangles

Children appreciate elegance of design, just as adults do. They sense its economy and the care given to detail. These simple sculptures are studies in understatement.

Preparation Instructions: Cut matte-board rectangles in many colors and sizes with a paper trimmer before class. The wider the color assortment, the better. Encourage a bit of thought about selecting harmonizing colors.

Make the largest about 8" long. Students will also need a little glue on paper scraps.

What You'll Need

- Matte board, assorted colors
- Pencils
- School glue

Directions

◆ Choose about five or six rectangles in harmonizing colors, and write your name on one.

◆ Stand a large rectangle on your work surface, slide an edge of another rectangle through the glue and press it, without pushing, against the side of the standing one, both bottom edges on the work surface, with one hand pushing from behind. Hold it for a few seconds, then release.

◆ Add the other rectangles the same way to these.

◆ You can make the sculpture vertical or horizontal; you can decide which direction at the outset or when it's finished and dry, by turning it different ways, even on its side, etc., to find the way you like best.

Salt

Make some rainbows in bottles with salt and food colors. They're almost mess-proof: students knead the salt and color together in self-sealing plastic bags and pour it into the bottles through holes cut in the bags. Clear or translucent bottles and jars such as those containing spices and baby-food juice work well. They hold about ½ cup (eight tablespoonfuls). Four-pound boxes of canning and pickling salt from supermarkets are the most economical.

Preparation Instructions: Before class, soak bottles containing labels in water for an hour or so and scrub off the labels (and the expiration date on baby-food juice bottles) with a kitchen scrubber and powdered cleanser.

When having students color the salt, as a general rule, one to three drops of color is about right for two tablespoonfuls of salt. As far as you're able, let children mix the colors to their specifications; however, more than four or five drops probably won't make much color difference and will make the salt too moist to pour from the plastic bags. They can start with one drop, knead it through the salt and decide if they want to add more. *Green food color usually needs an equal amount of yellow added to distinguish it from blue and brighten it: one drop yellow for each drop green. Additionally, yellow salt may require more color than the other colors.*

Put the salt in containers for students to share. Show them how much to put in the bags—about two tablespoonfuls (one ounce) of each color they plan to use may be about right, but you can adjust the amount of salt for the size of the bottles you use. Spice bottles and baby-food juice bottles hold about ½ cup, or eight tablespoonfuls. Students choose the colors they want to use. White salt separates the color bands and highlights the colors.

What You'll Need

- Bottles, clear or translucent, with caps
- Containers to hold the salt
- Food colors in dropper bottles
- Metal or plastic spoons, coffee measures or small scoops
- Scissors
- Small (sandwich size) self-sealing plastic bags
- Table salt

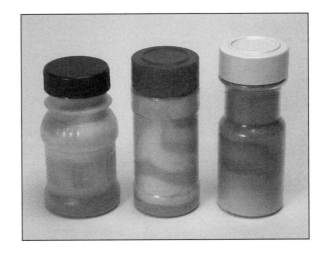

Directions

◆ Drop food coloring, drop by drop, slowly and deliberately, onto the salt in the bags and seal them immediately to prevent spilling.

◆ Knead the outside of the bags with your fingers to mix the colors throughout the salt until each is evenly colored.

◆ Then, holding the bag so the salt is in a lower corner, cut about ½" from the opposite lower corner with scissors and pour some or all of the salt into a bottle.

◆ Add other colors to the bottle to make bands of color in any order you choose. The layers will probably be slanted, which adds to their attractiveness. White salt can also be used to separate the colors, if you wish.

◆ You should tap your filled bottle on your work surface to settle the salt, then add more, since the salt will settle as it dries. Cap the bottle when you're finished.

Six Standing

When construction paper is folded, it will readily stand. These sculptures are quick and easy; urge students to give thought to the cutouts and arrangements, so the sculptures look good from several perspectives. They'll gain measuring experience by cutting their own rectangles.

Preparation Instructions: Cut construction paper in half crosswise, making 6" x 9" pieces for the sculpture bases, before class begins. Students need a little glue on paper scraps.

What You'll Need

- Construction paper, white and colored, 9" x 12"

- Pencils

- Rulers

- School glue

- Scissors

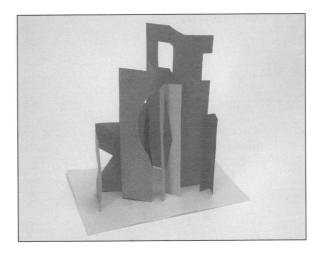

Directions

◆ Measure, mark and cut six rectangles out of scraps or sheets of construction paper of mixed colors and varying sizes, with the longest about 9".

◆ Fold the rectangles once or twice, vertically or horizontally, and make cutouts on some or all of the folds.

◆ Without using glue, stand the rectangles on the half-sheets of construction paper, then lift and refold them, dip the folded bottom edges in glue and gently replace them on the paper.

◆ The sculptures shouldn't be moved until the glue has set.

Skyscrapers

Children fit card-sized slotted styrofoam pieces together to make these sculptures, and learn a good deal about balance in the process. Pieces must be strategically placed to make the structure stand, but this is not difficult. Good-quality student scissors will cut the styrofoam.

Preparation Instructions: Cut the edges off the styrofoam trays before class begins.

What You'll Need

- Pencils
- Rulers
- Scissors
- Styrofoam, white and colored (see the Introduction)

Directions

◆ Measure and mark a rectangle about 2½" x 3½" on a piece of styrofoam, and cut it out.

◆ Cut two slots (four cuts in all) on one long side as wide as the styrofoam is thick to almost the center of the rectangle and pull out the small pieces between the cuts.

◆ Write your name or initials on it with pencil and mark around it, including inside the slots, 13 to 14 times on styrofoam in at least two colors.

◆ You can place the rectangles edge to edge to conserve styrofoam.

◆ Cut the pieces out and make cutouts on the unslotted long sides of some.

◆ Fit four rectangles together, slots in slots, to form a box base, then add the rest of the pieces, fitting the slots of some pieces on the unslotted edges of others, placing the pieces so they will balance the structure and it will stand.

◆ You should put some pieces on the sides to give it width.

Slots in Slots

Slotted constructions are fun to make—there's no one right way to make them. These sculptures are made of styrofoam pieces all cut alike. All the pieces but one are of one color.

Preparation Instructions: Cut the edges off the styrofoam trays before class begins and cut construction paper rectangles about 4" or 5" x 3", one per student. Students may need help to keep the sculpture from spreading too much horizontally; these need height.

What You'll Need

- Construction paper, white or colored
- Pencils
- Rulers
- Scissors
- Styrofoam, assorted colors and/or white (see the Introduction)

Directions

- Choose styrofoam in two colors. Cut shapes out of the construction paper rectangles as large as you can, using curves, angles, zigzags, etc.

- Mark around the shapes six or seven times on styrofoam of one color and once on styrofoam of a second color. Cut them out.

- Make two cuts (one slot), about as wide as the styrofoam is thick, into each piece about one-third of the way, varying the placement, and pull out the small pieces between the cuts.

- Fit pieces together, slots in slots, to make a vertical sculpture, repositioning pieces when necessary to achieve height.

Stick-Ups

These little sculptures seem to defy gravity—posterboard pieces stick together at right angles. This is a good time to use odd-sized pieces or scraps of posterboard.

Preparation Instructions: If you're using large pieces of posterboard, cut them into smaller pieces before class. Each piece students cut (not counting the base) must have at least one straight edge for gluing. Encourage them to make the other edges interesting. They can do some creative cutting and folding on some pieces, making fins, flaps, cutouts, etc., on some of the edges or folds. Students will also need a little glue on paper scraps.

What You'll Need

- Posterboard, assorted colors
- School glue
- Scissors

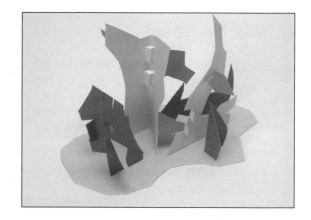

Directions

◆ Choose pieces of posterboard in several colors and cut an interesting shape about 6"–7" long and 3"–4" wide out of one for a base.

◆ Cut three or four large and medium pieces (not larger than the base) and some small (not over 2" or so) and tiny ones (1" or so). Each piece must have at least one straight edge for gluing. Make the other edges interesting—curved and angular, zigzag, wavy, scalloped, etc.

◆ Fold one of the large pieces, straight edge at the bottom, with bottom edges even—you can cut them if they're not even—and dip the folded bottom edge in glue and set it on the base. Beginning with a folded piece is a sure way to start; however, pieces can stand without being folded.

◆ If you want to start with an unfolded piece, dip a straight edge of a large/medium piece in glue and stand it on the base, supporting it for a few seconds and release. You should be sure the bottom of the piece (the edge with glue) is larger than the top, so it will stand.

◆ After placing the large/medium pieces on the base, dip a straight edge of small/tiny pieces in glue and stick them at right angles on the standing pieces and base. Some will stick with only a touch; others will need support. If they don't stick after being released, they probably have too much glue; you'll need to blot some glue on scrap paper and try again.

Straws and Clips

Straw-and-paper clip sculptures are best when they're large. Students like to work in pairs to make these.

What You'll Need

- Metal paper clips, about 1¼" long
- Plastic drinking straws (about 8" long, not flexible), assorted colors
- Masking tape (optional)
- Pencils (optional)

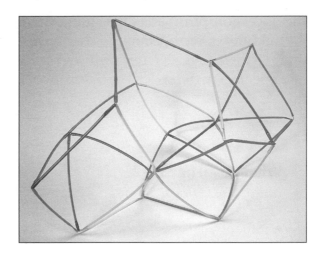

Directions

◆ Open paper clips by pulling the small rounded ends outward to form a letter "S" and spread the small ends slightly, so they will fit snugly in the straws. You can prepare more as you need them.

◆ Put clips in straws to connect them, putting several clips in each straw and bending the clips in any direction before or after inserting them. Think tall more than wide.

◆ Continue building, adding straws and clips where they will make the sculpture the strongest. Don't leave any straws unconnected.

◆ Turn your finished sculpture in different ways to find the way you like best. Write your name on masking tape and put it on the sculpture.

Sugar Cubes

Children of all ages love making these. Be sure to have plenty of sugar cubes on hand so the sculptures can be generously sized. A one-pound box will make two to three sculptures.

Preparation Instructions: Don't build these sculptures on newspaper or other paper, or they'll stick to it. Grade Levels 1–3 will tend to make simple chunky, box-like structures; help them see more possibilities than these. Grade Levels 4–5 can make more complex structures and add arches and openings—they'll have to make these separately from the main structure and add them to it after they've dried. They can begin the main structure, then make arches and openings at the end of the class period to be left to dry until the next one.

What You'll Need

- Pencils
- School glue
- Sugar cubes
- Brushes for glue (optional)

Directions

◆ Begin with experimentation: without using glue, try the sugar cubes in various placements.

◆ To stick cubes together, put a drop of glue or brush glue on one cube and stick it to another one and continue.

◆ Write your name or initials on the structure somewhere with pencil and allow it to dry before moving it.

Sugar Cube Mosaics

These mosaics are made with painted sugar cubes. Lighter weight backings than matte board won't work, but you can probably buy matte-board scraps inexpensively from a picture framer. These colorful mosaics are definitely worth the trouble of getting it.

What You'll Need

- Matte board, white and colored
- Paint brushes
- School glue
- Sugar cubes
- Tempera paint, assorted colors
- Water for washing brushes

Directions

◆ Without using glue, experiment by arranging unpainted sugar cubes on the matte board, leaving a bit of space between the cubes. Some possibilities are: a spiral or concentric circles arranged by color or randomly, a free-form shape, patterns, stripes or wavy or zigzag lines of alternating colors. The cubes shouldn't cover the entire board, but leave some space on all sides.

◆ When you've decided on an arrangement, remove the cubes and paint them, one side at a time, on five sides, leaving one side unpainted for gluing. *Dipping cubes in paint will partially dissolve them.*

◆ When the cubes are dry, place them on the matte board in your chosen arrangement, lift each cube in order, put a drop of glue or brush glue on its unpainted side and replace it on the board.

Triangles

These matte-board sculptures are quick to make. Talk with your class about triangles' properties: their only requirement is to have three sides; the proportions of the sides may vary. The more they vary for this project, the better.

Preparation Instructions: Buy matte-board scraps from a picture framer. Cut six to eight triangles of assorted colors per student before class, making them from about 6" long to very small. Students also need a little glue on paper scraps.

What You'll Need

- Matte board, assorted colors
- Pencils
- School glue

Directions

◆ Choose six to eight triangles of different sizes and colors and write your name on one.

◆ Stand a large triangle on one of its edges on the work surface, slide an edge of another triangle in the glue, then press the glued edge against one side of the standing piece, with its bottom edge against the work surface.

◆ Hold it a few seconds and release, then continue adding pieces until the sculpture is finished. Let sculptures dry in place before moving them.

Tubes

Cardboard bathroom tissue tubes provide unusual opportunities for experimenting with balance and design. They're a good example of art that can be made from everyday materials. These constructions are vertical and horizontal. Children make two arrangements.

Preparation Instructions: Before class time, cut construction paper in different colors into fourths, halved crosswise and lengthwise, remove any fragments of tissue from the tubes by rubbing them gently with a damp cloth or sponge, and cut them in half lengthwise with adult scissors. Students also need a little glue on paper scraps. Suggest symmetry and repeated patterns.

What You'll Need

- Cardboard bathroom tissue tubes
- Construction paper, colored, 12" x 18"
- School glue

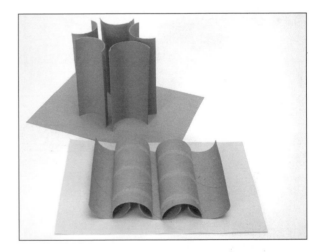

Directions

◆ Choose two construction paper pieces, in the same or different colors, and place four or more tube halves on the paper, vertically or horizontally, on cut edges, rounded sides or ends.

◆ Symmetrical placements will be more pleasing than random ones; you can try both to see for yourself.

◆ When you've decided on two arrangements, dip the edges, sides or ends of the tubes in glue, and replace them on the paper.

Wee Boxes

These little boxes open and close and are made on graph paper without measuring. Children are pleased and surprised to learn how boxes are made—six sides folded together. After making these they can make boxes of any size out of construction or other paper or card stock using a cardboard square as a pattern.

What You'll Need

- Broad-line markers, assorted colors
- Graph paper
- Pencils
- School glue
- Scissors

Directions

◆ With the graph paper placed vertically, draw around eight squares slightly above the center of the sheet (beginning with about the thirteenth square from the paper's left edge) in four directions on the lines with pencil to make the box's bottom.

◆ Draw around eight squares on all four of its sides and around eight more above the top square to make the box's lid.

◆ Draw one-square-wide flaps, three on the lid and two on each of the sides, as shown.

◆ Color and decorate the box with markers, cut it out and fold on the lines.

◆ Put dots of glue on the four side flaps, but not on the three lid flaps, and stick the glued flaps inside the box, leaving the lid free to be opened and closed.

Wings

These soaring shapes seem poised for flight, beautiful in their simplicity. They're made of folded index cards. Help students see that they work best in tight, sequential arrangements. Grades one and two may make one arrangement; grades three and four perhaps make three.

Preparation Instructions: Cut the colored construction paper before class time: for one arrangement, one 6" x 9" piece (half of a 9" x 12" sheet) for each student. For three, cut three 5" x 9" pieces, all the same color. The white base paper should be 9" x 12" for one arrangement, 12" x 18" for three. Students need a small amount of glue on paper scraps.

What You'll Need

- Construction paper, white, 12" x 18"
- Construction paper, white and colored, 9" x 12"
- Index cards, white, unruled, 3" x 5"
- School glue
- Scissors

Directions

◆ Fold index cards diagonally, one short end to one long side, edges matching exactly, and cut the bottoms off. You won't use the small end pieces.

◆ Glue the colored construction paper pieces to a sheet of white construction paper.

◆ Without using glue, place the folded cards on the colored paper and experiment with different sequential or repetitious arrangements.

◆ When you've decided on your arrangement(s), lift each card, dip a v-shaped edge in glue and set it lightly back in place.

Molas

Fabric molas are an important folk art in some countries. They're colorful appliqués of several layers of fabric. These paper molas are simplified versions of those.

Preparation Instructions: Have two students share four sheets of construction paper in four colors of their choice.

What You'll Need

- Construction paper, white and colored, 9" x 12"
- Pencils
- School glue
- Scissors

Directions

◆ Fold the construction paper in half crosswise and cut on the folds. Each of you uses four half-sheets, one of each color. Fold three of the pieces in half lengthwise, and cut a large shape (without drawing) on the fold of one. You may also cut a shape or shapes from the ends and/or sides if you want.

◆ Discard the cut-out pieces and put the folded negative (the piece the shape was cut from) on top of one of the other two folded pieces, mark about ¼" inside the cut edge or edges, and cut out the shape or shapes.

◆ Repeat these steps with the third folded piece. Then unfold and stack the three pieces on the uncut one, so that all the design edges show and all the outside edges are even. The last piece cut will be on the bottom.

◆ Glue the pieces together, then glue the mola to a sheet of construction paper.

Paper Weave

These designs look complex but are easy to make. They're made with a simple over-and-under technique; this project is a good introduction to weaving. Perhaps you can show your class some weavings or weaving pictures.

What You'll Need

- Construction paper, white and colored, 9" x 12"
- School glue
- Scissors

Directions

◆ Choose two sheets of construction paper in different colors.

◆ Cut one sheet in eight crosswise strips of different widths.

◆ Fold the other one in half crosswise, and make four wavy or zigzag cuts from the fold to about 1½" from the top edges.

◆ Weave the strips through the cuts, alternating over and under, sliding them upward as far as possible. You won't use all the strips, and you can cut the last one narrower to fit if necessary.

◆ Glue the ends of the strips to the paper.

Ribbons

You may want to combine this project with "Sticks," to give students a choice. If you plan to display them on a wall, students can glue them to paper.

Preparation Instructions: Buy as many different colors, textures, widths and patterns of ribbons as you can from a fabric or craft store. The more varied they are, the better, so the weavings will all be different. Before class, cut styrofoam rectangles about 6" or 7" x 8". If you're pairing this project with the "Sticks" project, cut them to 5" x 6" or 7". If you plan to display the weavings on a wall, students can glue them to either half-sheets or full sheets of 9" x 12" construction paper, depending on the size of the styrofoam used.

What You'll Need

- Pencils
- Ribbon
- Rulers
- Scissors
- Styrofoam, white and/or colored (see the Introduction)
- Yarn, assorted colors
- Construction paper, white and colored, 9" x 12" (optional)
- School glue (optional)

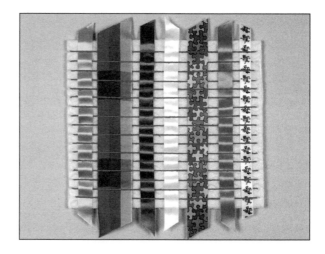

Directions

◆ Choose a styrofoam rectangle, write your name on it and use your scissor tips to make cuts in the two short sides—about ⅜" apart, the same number on both sides.

◆ Pull yarn through the first cut on one end, with the yarn end in back, through the corresponding cut at the opposite end on the front, to the back, through the next cut on the front and so on.

◆ When all the cuts are filled, cut the yarn on the back and tuck both ends under the yarn.

◆ Select, measure and cut some ribbon, in lengths a bit longer than the width of the styrofoam.

◆ Weave the ribbons through the yarn, letting them extend past the edges of the styrofoam.

Sticks

The sticks in these easy little weavings are wood ice cream sticks, also called "craft sticks." You can use recycled ones or buy them from teacher supply catalogs or craft stores. Pair this project with "Ribbons," if you like, and let students choose which to make. If you display the weavings on a wall, children can glue them to half-sheets of construction paper.

Preparation Instructions: Cut pieces of styrofoam which are about 5" x 6" or 7" before class. Before students begin weaving, talk about weaving possibilities with them: they can push one or more sticks at a time, over and under the strands of yarn; they can make the spaces between them even or uneven; they can skip some strands.

What You'll Need

- Pencils

- Scissors

- Styrofoam, white and/or colored (see the Introduction)

- Wood ice cream (craft) sticks, about 4" x ⅜"

- Yarn, assorted colors

- Construction paper, white or colored, 9" x 12" (optional)

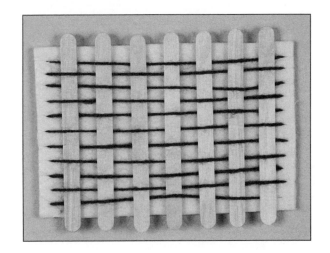

Directions

◆ Write your name on a styrofoam piece and make cuts in the two short ends with the tips of your scissors, about ⅜" apart, the same number on each side.

◆ Pull yarn through the first cut on one end, with the end of the yarn in back, through the corresponding cut at the opposite end on the front, to the back, through the next cut on the front and so on.

◆ When all the cuts are filled, cut the yarn on the back and tuck both yarn ends under the yarn strands.

◆ Weave sticks into the yarn: You can push one or more sticks over and under the strands of yarn. You can make the spaces between them even or uneven. You can skip some strands.

Straws

Children like the regularity and symmetry of weaving and these weavings are a good way to learn the process. Show them examples, if you can, of woven materials, including their own clothes. If you display these weavings on a wall, students can glue them to paper; otherwise, they can be left as they are. You'll find colored straws in supermarkets, craft stores and party shops.

Preparation Instructions: Cut pieces of styrofoam about 7" wide and 8" or 9" long before class begins. Before students begin weaving, discuss the possibilities with them: they can use straws of all colors or only two or three; they can mix colors randomly or use a repeating pattern; they can also vary the spacing between the straws.

What You'll Need

- Pencils

- Plastic drinking straws (about 8" long, not flexible), assorted colors

- Scissors

- Styrofoam, white and/or colored (see the Introduction)

- Yarn, assorted colors

- Construction paper, white or colored, 9" x 12" (optional)

- School glue (optional)

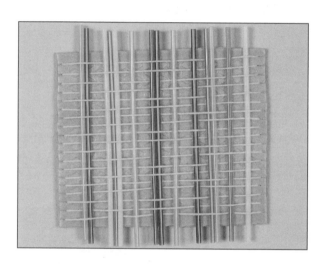

Directions

◆ Write your name on one piece of styrofoam and make cuts into the two short sides with the tips of your scissors, about ⅜" apart, the same number on each side.

◆ Pull yarn through the first cut on one end, with the end of the yarn in back, through the corresponding cut at the opposite end on the front, to the back, through the next cut on the front and so on. You can tie more yarn on the back as you need to.

◆ When all the cuts are filled, you cut the yarn on the back and tuck both yarn ends under the yarn strands.

◆ To weave, push one or more straws at a time through the yarn (the ends will extend past the styrofoam edges), over and under one or more strands, spacing them unevenly, perhaps, to add interest.

Discs

Like "Mystery Mobiles," these take shape when they're suspended. Some children say they look like bubbles or shells.

Preparation Instructions: Before class, cut cardboard circles (an easy way is to mark around a round object) which are 2½" to 3½" in diameter.

What You'll Need

- Clear tape
- Construction paper, white and colored
- Hole punch
- Lightweight cardboard
- Pencils
- Scissors
- String

Directions

◆ Mark around the circles with pencil on two colors of construction paper about fifteen times. Cut them out and cut a slit almost to the center of each.

◆ Then write your name on one circle, and, with the circles lying flat, fit the edges, not slits, of some circles in the slits of others, varying the placement, and put tape strips over the slits. *To prevent the mobile from being a long chain, don't put all the circles and slits opposite each other, and put two circles, perhaps joined, on some, then put a circle or two on them.*

◆ When all the circles are joined and taped, ask a classmate to hold your creation suspended while you bend the circles up where they're taped. Make a hole with the hole punch and tie string through for hanging.

Lanterns

These white globes are reminiscent of Japanese paper lanterns. They're made of construction paper circles, and look wonderful hanging in groups at different levels.

Preparation Instructions: Draw around a cup or glass that is approximately 3" in diameter to create cardboard circle patterns before class begins.

What You'll Need

- Construction paper, white, 9" x 12"
- Hole punch
- Lightweight cardboard
- Pencils
- School glue
- Scissors
- String

Directions

◆ Mark around cardboard circle patterns 20 times on construction paper, cut out the circles, and write your name or initials on one.

◆ Fold three equal-sized flaps on one circle, making sharp points—this is important. The three flaps must meet exactly.

◆ With the flaps folded flat, mark around the resulting triangle on the other 19 circles and fold them on the lines.

◆ To make the lanterns, glue the 20 circles together by the flaps so that five triangles meet at each corner.

◆ Make a hole in one flap and tie string through for hanging.

Mystery Mobiles

What these easy mobiles will look like is a mystery until they're suspended. They're made with white and colored index cards.

Preparation Instructions: Have students choose 12 to 14 cards in one or more colors of their choice.

What You'll Need

- Hole punch
- Index cards, white and assorted colors, unruled, 3" x 5"
- Pencils
- School glue
- String

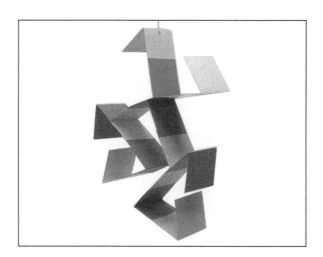

Directions

◆ Write your name on one of your index cards.

◆ Then, fold it in half crosswise, matching the corners and pressing the folds well.

◆ Put glue across one end of one card, press it to an end of another, and continue gluing cards to the ends and folds of other cards, making it branch out.

◆ When the glue is dry, hold the mobile up by different cards until you find the shape you like best.

◆ Make a hole with a hole punch in the card at the top of the chosen position, and tie string through the hole for hanging.

Snowflakes

After children learn to make snowflakes, they begin turning up everywhere. These big and fluffy double snowflakes are made by taping two identical single ones together. Children like to use single snowflakes to decorate gifts and make holiday decorations. Single or double, they can be made any size of any lightweight paper, including colored and metallic papers.

What You'll Need

- Clear tape
- Pencils
- Scissors
- String
- Typing, copier or other lightweight paper, about 8½" x 11"

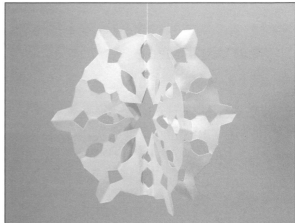

Directions

◆ Fold a sheet of paper diagonally, bringing a short end to a long side, edges exactly even, and cut the bottom off, making a folded triangle.

◆ With the fold of the triangle at the top, pull the two side points to the middle, one over the other until the top makes a sharp point and the side edges are exactly even—this is important.

◆ Fold this in half vertically, side folds together, pressing the fold firmly, and cut the tip (top) off, straight or slanting.

◆ Cut the bottom at a slant, in either direction, being sure to cut through all the layers. Cut large and small, round and/or pointed notches from the two sides and bottom.

◆ Without unfolding the snowflake, make another identical one, cutting it as nearly like the first one as possible.

◆ Unfold both snowflakes, cut one in half, and put one of the halves on the whole snowflake, matching the outside edges. Put a strip of tape on the center cut edge from top to bottom.

◆ Tape the other half on the back side of the snowflake, separate the four sections by bending them apart where they're taped.

Stuffed Animals

Create a classroom zoo—one that hangs from the ceiling, that is. The children can even name the animals if they want. Talk with them about the kinds of animals that would work for this activity: most any kind of plump-bodied animal, fish, bird or reptile. The animals require a lot of paint.

Preparation Instructions: If students are using paper bags, they cut the bottoms off, flatten them with their hands and cut them into two equal pieces, turning any writing inside. If they're using craft paper, they use two pieces about the size of a large paper bag.

What You'll Need

- Craft paper or large paper grocery bags
- Hole punch
- Newspapers
- Paint brushes
- Paper clips
- Pencils
- School glue
- Scissors
- String
- Tempera paint, assorted colors

Directions

◆ On one piece of brown paper, draw as large a plump-bodied animal, fish, reptile or bird as you can, and cut it out.

◆ Mark around the animal on the other piece, and cut it out. Put glue around the edge of one cut-out, leaving an opening for one of your hands, and stick the two pieces together.

◆ Paint both sides of the animal, realistically or imaginatively, covering it completely. Let it dry on newspapers.

◆ Push small pieces of crumpled newspaper into the opening to stuff the animal, then glue the opening closed (you may need to paper clip it until the glue dries). Make a hole with a hole punch and tie string through for hanging.

Birds

If you haven't discovered colored art tissue, you and your students are in for a treat. Its vibrant colors create jewel tones when a glue/water mixture is brushed over them on paper. Talk about birds before beginning this project—show pictures of various kinds and talk about their different shapes, but put the pictures away before beginning the project. Be sure the students' scissors are able to cut through the layers of tissue.

Preparation Instructions: Students need small containers of glue and water mixed equally, which they can share, working in pairs. They will share tissue, too. Save the tissue scraps for making other projects, including "Confetti."

What You'll Need

- Art tissue, assorted colors
- Brushes for glue
- Construction paper, white and colored
- Pencils
- School glue
- Scissors
- Water

Directions

◆ Stack four or five sheets of tissue of related colors (in the same color family or harmonizing colors) of your choice, edges even.

◆ Fold one end (a short side) of the stack up about 4", crease, cut beside the edges and put the rest of the tissue aside for future projects.

◆ Leaving the tissue folded, fold it end to end and cut the stack in half crosswise on the crease. Each of you in your pair takes half the tissue.

◆ Draw two large birds (alike or different and without legs) on the top sheet of folded tissue, making them about 3½" to 4", and cut them out, cutting through all the layers at once.

◆ Place the birds, one at a time, on white or colored construction paper (your choice) and brush the glue/water mixture over them, brushing from the center outward, being sure to stick all the edges. It's alright if the colors bleed.

◆ Adhere all the birds, facing either or both directions, randomly and overlapping.

Cityscapes

Your class will be surprised and delighted at being able to make these impressive paintings. They make them on half-sheets of posterboard, stamping the buildings with painted cardboard rectangles and finishing them with markers. They may add people, vehicles and animals, or not.

Preparation Instructions: Cut the posterboard in half across to make 14" x 22" pieces before class begins. Cut cardboard rectangles in three sizes—small, medium and large, the large size about 8" x 3". Before students finish the paintings, spend a few minutes talking about details they can add: arches, doorways, windows, towers, signs, etc. They can add people, animals, vehicles—their choice.

What You'll Need

- Broad-line markers, assorted colors
- Lightweight cardboard
- Paint brushes
- Pencils
- Posterboard, white and assorted colors, 22" x 28"
- Tempera paint, assorted colors
- Water for washing brushes

Directions

◆ Choose a piece of posterboard for the base.

◆ Brush black and white paint on one rectangle of cardboard, covering it completely. It's all right if the colors mix slightly. *It's a good idea to have brushes for both colors of paint.*

◆ Press the painted side of the rectangle, vertically and horizontally, in several places on the posterboard, adding paint as needed. Paint and stamp the same way with the other two rectangles, crowding and overlapping the painted rectangles, turning some vertically, some horizontally, covering most of the posterboard.

◆ Put a small amount of black paint on a paper scrap, slide one edge of the small or medium cardboard rectangle in the paint, and stamp the painted edge lightly, without bending, to outline parts of some or all of the buildings.

◆ Stamp some rooflines, poles, antennas, etc.

◆ Let the paintings dry before finishing them with markers, adding windows, doors, arches, towers, signs, etc. You may add people, animals, vehicles, etc.

Confetti

Colored art tissue is easy for even the youngest children to use. They brush a glue/water mixture over it to adhere it to paper and it dries semi-transparent. This torn tissue collage is made with small pieces of tissue—scraps left from making the "Birds" project, if you wish.

Preparation Instructions: Put equal parts glue and water in the small cups before class time for students to share.

What You'll Need

- Art tissue, assorted colors
- Brushes for glue
- Construction paper, white and colored, 9" x 12" and 12" x 18"
- School glue
- Scissors
- Small cups
- Water

Directions

◆ Tear tissue into small pieces, about 1"–2", without crumpling them and place them, one at a time, on 9" x 12" white or colored construction paper of your choice.

◆ Brush the glue/water mixture over the tissue pieces, completely covering and overlapping them, adhering the edges well. The tissue should cover the paper completely and extend past the edges where necessary. It's all right if the colors bleed.

◆ When the glue is dry, trim the edges and glue the collages on 12" x 18" white or colored paper.

Diamonds

This abstract graphic contains three sizes of diamonds—small, medium and large; the spaces are colored with markers.

Preparation Instructions: Before class begins, cut the cardboard diamonds in three sizes: about 1", 2" and 2½" tall. Cut some construction paper in half across.

What You'll Need

- Broad-line markers, assorted colors
- Construction paper, white and colored, 9" x 12"
- Lightweight cardboard
- Pencils
- School glue
- Scissors

Directions

◆ Select diamonds from all three sizes and a half-sheet and full sheet of your choice of either white or colored construction paper.

◆ Mark around the three diamonds, mixing the sizes, with pencil on the half-sheet of paper (turned in either direction), turning the diamonds lengthwise and/or crosswise and overlapping them so they're all connected.

◆ Make about three or four or more of each size, then color the spaces with markers, coloring each space a different color and leaving some spaces uncolored if you wish. Colors may be repeated.

◆ Glue the pictures on the full sheets of white or colored construction paper—your choice.

Dips

These designs are fast, easy and always a surprise. They're made with food coloring and paper towels.

Preparation Instructions: Students can share the food colors and cups or muffin tins. Put a tablespoonful of water in each cup or muffin tin cup before class.

What You'll Need

- Construction paper, white and colored, 12" x 18"
- Food coloring in dropper bottles
- Newspapers
- Paper towels, white, without printing
- Pencils
- Plastic teaspoons
- Rulers
- School glue
- Small cups or muffin tins

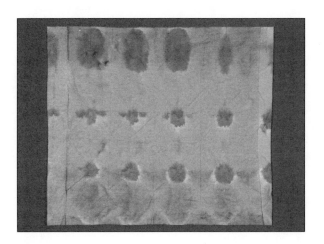

Directions

◆ Put one to three drops of each of three food colors in your cups and stir.

◆ With the short ends of a paper towel at the top and bottom, measure with your ruler and make pencil marks 2" from the bottom edge on each side of the towel and fold on the marks, creasing the fold well.

◆ Make a fold the same size (without measuring) in the opposite direction, then reverse and fold, alternating directions, like a fan, to the other end of the towel. It may not come out even.

◆ With the folded towel vertically on the work surface, fold the bottom left corner diagonally—even with the opposite edge and crease it well.

◆ Fold this triangular section to the back and crease, then to the front, continuing to alternate to the end of the towel (it's alright if it doesn't come out even). You should end up with a stacked triangle.

◆ Dip the folded corners briefly in the colored water, each corner in a different color, leaving some white space in the center.

◆ Carefully unfold the picture to dry on newspaper, then glue it to construction paper in a color that complements the picture.

Doubles

Children utilize the concept of positive and negative with these construction paper designs. The positive parts are the cut shapes and the negative parts are the spaces they were cut from.

Preparation Instructions: Cut some construction paper into half-sheets (cut crosswise) before class begins.

What You'll Need

- Construction paper, white and colored, 9" x 12"
- Pencils
- School glue
- Scissors

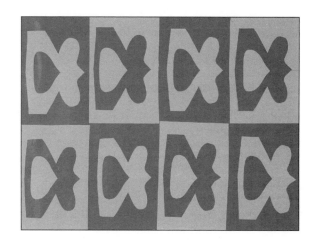

Directions

◆ Choose a full sheet and half-sheet of paper in different colors.

◆ Fold the half-sheet in half crosswise and in half again (fold to fold), unfold it and cut on the creases, making four 3" x 4½" pieces.

◆ Fold the four pieces in half crosswise and cut, without drawing, a large shape on the fold of one, and cut a small shape out of it.

◆ Refold the large shape, mark around it on each of the three other folded pieces, and cut them out.

◆ Draw around the small shape on the three large shapes, and cut them out.

◆ Glue all the pieces, positives and negatives, to the full sheet, alternating positives and negatives, with cut shapes (positives) inside the negative spaces.

Drops

These designs emerge before children's eyes. They drop diluted food colors on paper towels to make random designs and finish them with markers. Let them mix the food coloring and water; don't prepare it beforehand, as it's part of the experience.

Preparation Instructions: Before class, put one tablespoon of water in each cup or muffin tin cup. Students can share them and the droppers.

What You'll Need

- Broad-line markers, assorted colors
- Construction paper, white and colored, 12" x 18"
- Food coloring in dropper bottles
- Medicine droppers, plastic
- Newspapers
- Paper towels, white, without printing
- School glue
- Small cups or muffin tins

Directions

◆ Put two drops of each of two food colors in two cups containing water, and stir with the medicine droppers.

◆ Drop colored water from both cups on paper towels, one drop at a time—slowly—putting the drops close together so they'll merge but not cover the towels—some white spaces should show. Let the pictures dry on newspaper.

◆ Outline some of the designs with colored and/or black markers. You can also add people, animals, buildings, etc., if the picture suggests them and you want to.

◆ Glue the finished picture to construction paper.

Flags

This marker graphic is not difficult; it's made without measuring—children mark above and below their rulers in both directions to make the grid lines. They halve the resulting squares diagonally and color half of each square to make patterns of their own design. Discuss possible patterns with the students: they can use any colors and any patterns or color the squares randomly; they can alternate two or more colors or rows.

What You'll Need

- Broad-line markers, assorted colors
- Construction paper, white, 9" x 12"
- Pencils
- Rulers
- Scissors

Directions

◆ With the paper turned either vertically or horizontally, place your ruler even with the top edge and mark beneath it, move it even with the lines and mark beneath it, repeating to fill the page.

◆ Turn the paper and repeat the process, making a grid. You should have five rows in one direction, six in the other.

◆ Trim the excess paper along the last lines and divide the squares, one at a time, with diagonal lines (without rulers).

◆ Color one of each of the halves with markers, either the top or bottom, for the entire picture, or skip some squares.

◆ Glue the completed picture to a full sheet of white construction paper.

Four by Four

These pictures are also puzzles—colored index cards are cut into fourths and reassembled.

Preparation Instructions: Give each student five index cards: one white, four colored, each a different color.

What You'll Need

- Construction paper, white, 9" x 12"
- Index cards, white and assorted colors, unruled, 3" x 5"
- Pencils
- School glue
- Scissors

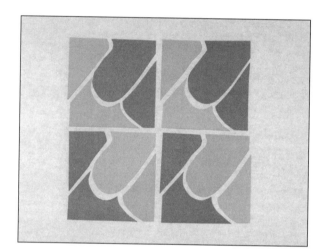

Directions

◆ Fold the white card diagonally, one short end to one long side, edges matching exactly, and cut the bottom off.

◆ Unfold the resulting square, place it on each of the colored cards, mark beside it with pencil, and cut on the lines. Put the white card aside; you won't use it or the small ends of the colored cards.

◆ Cut one square in four different-sized pieces, reassemble and mark around them on each of the other three cards, and cut the pieces apart.

◆ Without using glue, reassemble the four cards on white construction paper sheets, leaving a bit of space between the pieces and between the squares, using each of the colors in each square, and orienting the pieces the same way in all of the squares.

◆ Glue the pieces in place.

One Color

Children like to mix colors, and they rarely feel they have enough opportunity to do so. That's what they do with these paintings—mix white with a color to make four different shades.

Preparation Instructions: Cut construction paper rectangles 1½" x 6" before class. There's probably no need to wash brushes between changing shades.

What You'll Need

- Construction paper, white and colored, 9" x 12"
- Paint brushes
- Paint sticks or craft sticks
- Palettes or paper plates
- Pencils
- Rulers
- Tempera paint, assorted colors
- Water for washing brushes

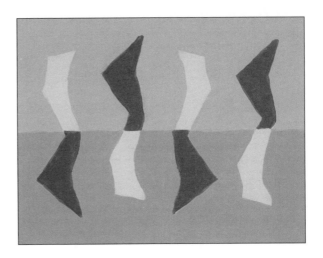

Directions

◆ Cut, without drawing or folding, the largest curved or angular shape you can from the small construction paper rectangles.

◆ Draw a pencil line down the lengthwise center of white construction paper (4½" from either side), using a ruler, and mark around the cut shape on the center line in four orientations: left and right of center, ends reversed, face up, face down on the paper.

◆ Mentally divide the drawing in four parts and paint one part white, then a part with a color (any color except yellow) in its original intensity.

◆ Lighten the color by adding white to it with a paint stick on the palette or paper plate and paint another part. Lighten it more, and paint the last part. There should be four distinct color hues.

Prisms

Children are fascinated by prisms. These marker pictures look a bit like prisms. They require measuring, but only a little, and offer good experience with rulers.

Preparation Instructions: Cut some of the paper in half (crosswise) before class begins.

What You'll Need

- Broad-line markers, assorted colors
- Construction paper, white, 9" x 12"
- Pencils
- Rulers
- School glue
- Scissors

Directions

◆ Turn half-sheets of construction paper so the long edges are at the sides, place your ruler even with the top edge and mark with pencil beneath the ruler.

◆ Move your ruler even with the line, mark below it and repeat this six times, making a total of eight lines. Cut on the last line.

◆ With your ruler even with the top edge of the paper, make a pencil mark at three inches, repeat on the bottom edge, and draw a line between them, dividing the paper in half.

◆ Using your ruler, mark diagonally from corner to corner through the top two spaces, making an "X."

◆ Skip the next space (a ruler's width) and repeat, making an "X" in the next two spaces, skip a space and make an "X" in the last two spaces. Erase the pencil lines in the two empty spaces.

◆ Color the spaces with markers in four colors (the same four colors for the entire picture), using each color twice in each of the three designs.

◆ Glue the completed design to 9" x 12" white construction paper.

Squares

Graph paper may be new to your students, but they'll quickly see its creative potential. This project's repeating patterns are made by coloring in some squares with markers. Demonstrate the process, perhaps on a chalkboard, to start ideas flowing, then let them come up with their own patterns.

Preparation Instructions: Trim off the edge of the graph paper that has holes. An interesting variation of this project is large designs, symmetrical or free-form, one to a page. For these, students may want to halve some squares diagonally in addition to coloring whole spaces to increase the design possibilities.

What You'll Need

- Broad-line markers, assorted colors
- Construction paper, white and colored, 9" x 12"
- Graph paper
- School glue
- Scissors

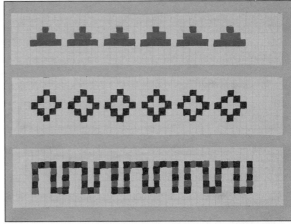

Directions

◆ Turn your graph paper in either direction.

◆ Color in squares to make repeating patterns.

◆ Make three or more rows of different patterns, leaving some empty spaces between them.

◆ Cut the rows apart, leaving two or three rows of blank spaces above and below the patterns, and glue them to white or colored construction paper.

Stripes

The most important part of this activity is making the bands of color. Children observe the progression beginning with yellow through the color spectrum and returning to yellow. Talk with them about the colors' relationships: for example, the two colors most closely related to yellow (orange and green), to red (orange and blue), to blue (purple and green), to green (yellow and blue), etc.

Preparation Instructions: Cut construction paper into half sheets (6" x 9"). Notice the size of the index cards is 4" x 6", not 3" x 5", as in other projects.

What You'll Need

- Broad-line markers, assorted colors
- Construction paper, black, 9" x 12"
- Index cards, white, unruled, 4" x 6"
- Pencils
- Rulers
- School glue
- Scissors

Directions

◆ With an index card turned horizontally (long edges at the top and bottom), place your ruler near the top and bottom edges and make light pencil marks at ½" intervals, but don't draw lines to connect them.

◆ Color 12 stripes with markers, using the half-inch marks as guides, in this order, making the sequence twice: yellow, orange, red, purple, blue and green. The stripes should touch, covering the card completely.

◆ On the reverse side of the card, with the card horizontal (long sides at the top and bottom), place your ruler even with the top edge and mark with pencil beside the bottom of the ruler across the card.

◆ Place the ruler even with the pencil line and mark beneath it. Repeat this once more, making three lines.

◆ Then, turn the card vertically and make five lines the same way; then trim the card on the last line in both directions.

◆ Cut on the grid lines and arrange the 15 blocks, without using glue, on a piece of black construction paper in either rows of three or five, a circle, staggered (offset) rows or some other arrangement, leaving a uniform amount of space between them, then glue them in place.

Windows

These marker pictures look like stained glass. Most children have seen stained glass windows.

Preparation Instructions: Show your class pictures of some stained glass windows if you can.

What You'll Need

- Broad-line markers, assorted colors
- Construction paper, white, 9" x 12"
- Pencils
- School glue

Directions

◆ Make back-and-forth pencil lines on the paper, beginning at one edge and going to another side or end.

◆ Without lifting your pencil, continue until the paper is criss-crossed with lines. Each line should go from one edge to another.

◆ Color all the spaces with markers, using all colors except black, then outline the spaces with a broad black line.

Apples

Have an apple day! Enjoy a snack of apple slices or cider with your class while they watch you halve the apples for this project. If it's apple harvest time where you live, so much the better. Cut the apples from stem to blossom ends. For a future project, you can cut them crosswise and the class can make all-over random prints or rows of apple prints with star-shaped centers.

Preparation Instructions: Cut 5" squares of white and colored construction paper before class time.

What You'll Need

- Apples
- Broad-line markers, black
- Construction paper, white and colored, 12" x 18"
- Paint brushes
- Paper towels
- School glue
- Tempera paint, assorted colors
- Water for washing brushes

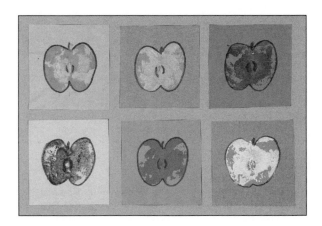

Directions

◆ Choose six squares of paper in six colors. Brush paint on an apple half and press it on a paper square without slapping or twisting. Then, wipe the paint off the apple with a paper towel and wash the brush.

◆ Use a different color of paint for each of the paper squares, then outline the apples and make stems and seeds with black markers.

◆ Glue the six prints to a sheet of 12" x 18" white or colored construction paper of your choice.

Oranges

Orange halves with alternating segments removed make beautiful starburst prints. If you have any reason to celebrate oranges (or none whatsoever), you can have an orange event: make these and drink orange juice to highlight the occasion.

Preparation Instructions: Before class time, cut the oranges in half crosswise (between the two ends) and, using a small knife, cut and remove about ¼" of every other segment. (They may not come out even.)

What You'll Need

- Broad-line markers, assorted colors
- Construction paper, white and colored, 9" x 12"
- Oranges, small to medium-sized
- Paint brushes
- School glue
- Tempera paint, assorted colors
- Water for washing brushes

Directions

◆ Choose white or colored construction paper and two paint colors.

◆ Brush paint on the oranges, one or two colors at a time, and print, without slapping, twisting or squeezing, several times on the paper, adding paint as you need to.

◆ You should fill the paper, overlapping and crowding the prints.

◆ When the pictures have dried, add marker details such as outlining or other details that the starbursts may suggest to you.

Squashed

Acorn squash may be new to your students and possibly to you. It's a relative of pumpkins, cucumbers and melons. Halved crosswise, squash slices make scalloped crescent prints. Cut the rings from several squash before class, but show your students a whole and half squash with the seeds in place, too. They can share the crescents.

Preparation Instructions: Before class begins, cut two slices about 1" thick from the centers of each of the squash between the stem and blossom ends. Remove the seeds from the rings, and cut them in half, making crescents. Help students design their prints: will they have overlapping chains? Rows of connected semi-circles? A page of scalloped concentric circles?

What You'll Need

- Acorn squash

- Construction paper, white and colored, 12" x 18"

- Paint brushes

- Paper towels

- Tempera paint, assorted colors

- Water for washing brushes

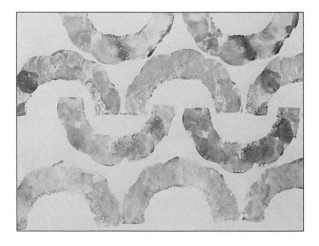

Directions

◆ Choose one to three colors of paint, brush it on the squash crescent, and press it on the paper without twisting. Add paint as you need to.

◆ Wash your brush and clean the squash with paper towels as you need to.

◆ You can put more than one color of paint at a time on the squash.

Cut Letters

Everybody should know how to cut paper letters—it's so handy. Learn how yourself, teach your students, and you'll all make them for years to come.

Preparation Instructions: Cut letters start with paper blocks all the same size, which automatically makes them uniform in size and appearance. They can be any size; square or rectangle. These are 2½" square, which is a good size for learning. Plan to spend several sessions on them, teaching a few at a time.

Cut construction paper into 2½" wide strips with a paper trimmer before class begins. Color is unimportant; the letters can even be of mixed colors.

Two variations of square letters, "Tall and Wide Cut Letters" and "Decorated Cut Letters" (see below) are fun to do when students have learned the basic cutting technique. You can follow this project with them, or do them at a later date.

Tall and Wide Cut Letters
These letters are made the same way as square letters, except they're cut from rectangles instead of squares. Students hold the rectangles vertically to cut Tall Letters and horizontally to cut Wide Letters. They can be any size, depending on the space they're to be used for, but 2" x 4" is good for learning. Teach students how to measure and cut the rectangles, so they can do it on their own later. Students can make the full alphabet of "Tall and Wide Cut Letters" or only some, at your discretion. Either way, they can make their names and any other words they or you suggest.

Decorated Cut Letters
Students can decorate any style of cut letters—square, tall or wide—with marker stripes, dots, little designs or holes made with a hole punch. Let them cut and mount their names or other words.

What You'll Need

- Construction paper, white or colored, 12" x 18"
- Pencils
- Rulers
- School glue
- Scissors
- Small self-sealing plastic bags
- Optional: Yardsticks or meter sticks, hole punch and broad-line markers, assorted colors

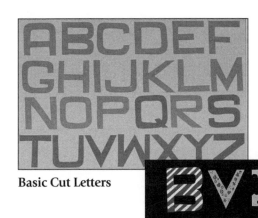

Basic Cut Letters

Decorated Cut Letters

Directions

◆ Use a ruler and pencil to measure, mark and cut a 2½" square from one strip of paper to use as a pattern, and mark it somehow so you won't make a letter with it. Place it on the strips, mark beside it, and cut on the lines to make squares.

◆ These letters are uppercase only. You should cut three (or more if necessary) of each letter and keep the best one in the self-sealing plastic bag, discarding the other letters, until you have a complete alphabet.

◆ Rounding the corners of the paper blocks is key—spend time on this. Corners should be uniformly rounded, but the letters should look like rounded blocks, not circles.

◆ All parts of the letters are the same width. This is important. For the letters in this project, the width is about ½".

◆ J and I don't have serifs.

◆ N and Z are made the same way; W and M are made the same way.

◆ To find the center of the top or bottom edge of a block, pinch (crease) it very lightly, bringing the corners together—handy for H, T, V, Y, X.

◆ The centers of A, B, E, F, G, H, K, R, X must be at the midpoint of the blocks.

◆ S is tricky, but you can master it.

◆ To cut inside circles (for example C and O) cut in to about the center of the square, then turn the square as you turn the scissors.

◆ When you have a complete alphabet, make light pencil marks on both short ends of 12" x 18" white or colored construction paper at 4", 7" and 10" from the top and connect them with lines. Glue the bottoms of the letters on the lines, slits closed (not overlapped) as they're glued on. You can spell your name with cut letters on separate paper if you'd like.

Fun & Fancy Letters

Novelty letters like these will find many homes after your class learns how to make them—on posters, booklets, bulletin boards and other projects. Explain that the letters are lowercase only and it's all right to use them even for proper names, since they're for special effects. They can be any size, but 2" circles and 4" straight pieces are a good size for learning. Plan to teach them in more than one session; keep the letters in self-sealing bags until they're all made.

Preparation Instructions: Before class begins, cut 2" diameter cardboard rounds (mark around an object that size); students can share them. Cut 6" squares in eight or more colors of construction paper.

What You'll Need

- Construction paper, white and colored, 12" x 18"
- Lightweight cardboard
- Pencils
- Rulers
- School glue
- Scissors
- Small self-sealing plastic bags
- Yardsticks or meter sticks (optional)

Directions

- Mark around cardboard circles with pencil seven times on construction paper squares of one color (four on each square), four times on a second color and twice on each of two other colors.

- Clear away paper scraps now and periodically later to avoid mixing letters and scraps. Keep cut letter parts in the plastic bags.

- Cut the circles out and cut into them almost to the center, then about ½" from the outside edge to make rings, discarding the centers.

◆ Leave seven rings of one color whole; fold the four of a second color in half at the slit and cut on the crease, making eight half-circles.

◆ Fold two rings of a third color in half twice and cut a quarter from them (using the slit as one cut), making three-quarter circles (discard the quarters).

◆ Fold and cut the two rings of a fourth color in fourths, making eight quarters. Discard one of the quarters; you will use only seven.

◆ To make the straight pieces, use a ruler and pencil to make seven marks at ½" intervals across the tops and bottoms of a square in a fifth color. Then, connect the marks with lines and cut on the lines, making seven ½" x 6" pieces. You won't use the remainder of the square of this fifth color. Leave these seven pieces whole.

◆ Mark and cut seven more pieces the same way on a square of a sixth color, fold them in half crosswise (ends matching) and cut on the creases, making 14 half-pieces. You will use only 13 of them, so discard one.

◆ Mark and cut four straight pieces of a seventh color, fold and cut them in half and in half again, making 16 quarter-pieces. Discard two, leaving 14.

◆ Mark and cut five pieces of an eighth color, fold one in half twice and cut one quarter off it, then use it as a guide to cut quarters off the other four, making five three-quarter pieces, discarding the quarters cut from them.

◆ Cut two ½" dots, one for the "j" and one for the "i" from a paper scrap of any of the colors used.

◆ Before mounting the letters on paper, check to see that you have all the letter parts:

Circles:	Straight Pieces:
Whole—7	Whole—7
Three-quarter—2	Three-quarter—5
Half—7	Half—13
Quarter—7	Quarter—14

◆ To mount the letters on paper, turn two white construction paper sheets lengthwise (long ends at the top and bottom), and make pencil marks on the short ends at 5" and 9½" from the top. If possible, use yardsticks or meter sticks; they are more efficient than rulers in this case. Then, connect the marks with light pencil lines to make horizontal lines.

◆ Without using glue, assemble the cut letter pieces of about the first seven letters ("a" through "g") on the line which is 5" from the top, on one sheet. Leave the pieces in place and turn each piece over, put glue on it and glue it in place. Straight pieces should be glued on top of circles, covering slits where they occur. Continue with the other letters, making "h" through "n" on the second line, "o" through "u" on the top line of the second sheet and "v" through "z" on the last line.

Lettering

Lettering is such a useful thing to know—people who learn it well as children use it all their lives. Your students can letter posters, booklets, reports and many other things. Plan to spend several sessions on these, teaching several letters each session.

Preparation Instructions: Demonstrate each letter's formation on a chalkboard, going slowly, beginning with "A" and proceeding through the alphabet, doing a few each class session. Students make each letter three times (or more if necessary) before going to the next one. You can follow this project with "Tall and Wide Lettering" and "Slant Lettering" (see below) or do them later. Children like making these exaggerated variations and they're not difficult—the letter formations are the same, only the guideline spacing or slant is different. There's probably no need for them to do the entire alphabet with these variations; teach them how to make a few letters and they can letter their names, and, if possible, other things for their classroom.

Tall and Wide Lettering
"Tall and Wide Letters" use widely or narrowly spaced pencil guidelines. The center of the letters may be centered between the lines or above or below the center for special effects, as shown.

Slant Lettering
"Slant Letters" can be either block (square), tall or wide; they can slant left or right. The only rule is this: the first downward strokes (vertical lines—look at B, D, E, e.g.) of all the letters must be parallel—at the same degree of slant. The other parts of the letters will automatically be parallel if the first downward strokes are. Children quickly catch on to this and enjoy its challenge.

What You'll Need

- Broad-line markers, black

- Pencils

- Rulers

- White typing or copier paper, or any unlined paper

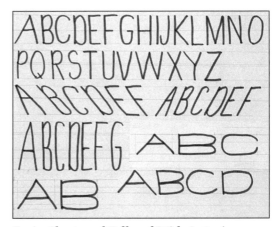

Basic, Slant, and Tall and Wide Lettering

Directions

Marker lettering is done between pencil guidelines, ensuring uniformity. The lines can be erased from finished projects. Letters about one inch tall are a good size for learning, but they can be any size for any size space, by adjusting the spacing of the guidelines.

◆ On paper, make pairs of guidelines which are a bit more than an inch apart by marking below your ruler (with the long sides of the paper at the top and bottom, place your ruler even with the top edge and mark along the bottom edge of the ruler). Repeat this five times, making a total of six lines.

◆ To make center guidelines for the centers of the letters, place your ruler at the estimated center of the first pair of lines and make a line, skip the next space and repeat, skip a space and repeat, making three sets of guidelines. You need to prepare at least two sheets this way before beginning lettering; you can do more as needed.

◆ When you've made the entire alphabet, make a final sheet with one of each letter and letter your name.

© 2002, LaBritta Gilbert, UpstartBooks

Posters

Here's where your class can use the lettering and letter-cutting skills they learned in the "Lettering," "Cut Letters" and "Fun and Fancy Letters" projects. Be sure they've learned them before doing this project. These posters can publicize an actual school function and be displayed, or they can be only pretend. Plan to spend several class periods making them.

Preparation Instructions: Guide students in selecting a title for a real or imaginary event—usually two to four words—and other information the poster will convey as well as a general mental picture of what it will look like. Also, help them decide what size the letters should be—usually 2" to 3" for square letters, 2" x 4" or smaller for rectangle ones and possibly 2" circles and 4" straight pieces for "Fun and Fancy Letters," although they can be smaller.

Lead them in cutting strips, then blocks, using rulers: have them make pencil marks at the top and bottom edges (lengthwise) of the paper, connect them with lines and cut on the lines to make strips, then cut one square or rectangle, and use it as a pattern to cut the rest. If they're using "Fun and Fancy Letters," they can draw around an object to make the circles the right size and make straight pieces twice as tall as the circles.

Help students decide where to put information (actual or pretend) such as the date, time, cost (if any), and any other information pertinent to the event.

What You'll Need

- Broad-line markers, assorted colors
- Construction paper, white and colored
- Erasers
- Posterboard, white and colored, 22" x 28"
- School glue
- Scissors
- Pencils
- Rulers
- Yardsticks or meter sticks (optional)

Directions

◆ Choose your posterboard and either white or colored construction paper for cut letters for the poster's title. Decide what kind of cut letters to use—square, tall, wide, fun and fancy, decorated, etc.

◆ Place the number of paper blocks needed for the title on the posterboard to be sure they fit, and make adjustments if necessary.

◆ Cut the blocks into letters and place them on the posterboard, without glue, leaving small places between them, on pencil guidelines made with rulers or yardsticks or meter sticks if the title will be in a straight line or sketched freehand if it will be curved. The posterboard can be turned in either direction.

◆ When the letters are arranged, glue them to the posterboard.

◆ Letter the date, time, cost (if any), and any other information lightly in pencil on the posterboard, if it's white or light-colored, using guidelines, or on a piece or pieces of colored or white construction paper with guidelines if the posterboard is a dark color. (You will glue it to the posterboard later.)

◆ Make marker (black or colored) letters over the pencil ones. If the lettering is on separate paper, glue it to the posterboard, perhaps putting a larger piece of white or colored construction paper behind it to frame it.

◆ Small drawings or cutouts add the posters' finishing touches. You can make drawings with markers on separate paper and cut them out or make construction paper cutouts—perhaps sports equipment for a sports event, musical notes or instruments for a musical one, books or science equipment for book or science fairs, etc.

◆ Glue the cutouts on the poster, and erase all pencil lines.